Katrin

Guinea Pigs

A Complete Pet Owner's Manual

Everything about
Purchase, Care, Nutrition,
Grooming, Behavior, and
Training

Photographs by Karin Skogstad

Illustrations by György Jankovics

BARRON'S

2 CONTENTS

TYPICAL
GUINEA PIG

- **Well padded**
- **Eyes bright and alert**
- **Fur of many colors, textures, and lengths**
- **Gentle and trusting**
- **Always ready to eat**
- **Needs wood for chewing**
- **Sociable**
- **Develops early**
- **Ready to reproduce early**

Guinea pigs originally arrived in the United States from South America. The "pig" in their name stuck because of their grunting and squeaky sounds. Children have adored them as pets because they love to be cuddled, don't scratch or bite, and thrive on company. Two guinea pigs can get along without fighting, even over food. They are surprisingly agile despite their chubbiness. They love to climb and enjoy the view from on high. Newborn guinea pigs are fully developed, able to run, and eager for solid food.

HOW TO CHOOSE

1 Guinea pigs live as long as eight to ten years. Make sure you are ready for a long-term commitment.

2 Guinea pigs need a large cage, which can be costly. Or you can construct a habitat for your new pet. This takes time.

3 The cage must be kept clean at all times, and the food must always be fresh. This also involves expense and time.

4 Guinea pigs are companionable animals, and they need daily attention and human interaction.

5 If the animal runs around in your living room there will be little puddles, some fecal trails, and the mark of teeth on furniture. You will need patience and tolerance.

6 As an adult you will be largely responsible for the guinea pig, even if you give it to your child as a gift.

7 Who will take care of the animal during your vacation, or while you are ill?

8 Guinea pigs can get ill. Will you be able to afford veterinary bills? Will someone be at home to care for them?

9 Do you have house pets that might not get along with a guinea pig addition?

10 Before you purchase a guinea pig, make sure that no family member is allergic to animal hair or dander. (page 51).

Singles or Doubles?

Guinea pigs are social animals that live in family groups in their natural setting. This should be sufficient reason to keep several guinea pigs.

✔ Single animals might be suitable for a child who needs a good pet and playmate. If, however, homework or other school activities don't allow enough time for the guinea pig, you should get another guinea pig to serve as company (page 21).

✔ Buying a pair should be for breeding purposes only (page 35). This choice could result in four to five litters per year. What would you do with all the young?

✔ Two females usually get along well with each other (page 21).

✔ Two immature males may be housed in one cage as long as they are brothers or have been together since they were a few days old. They also may be housed together if they are males who have had no contact with females since they reached sexual maturity. You may also add a young male as companion for an older male guinea pig. Do not place two unacquainted adult males together. This will not work even if one or both are neutered.

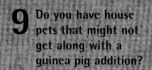

GETTING ACQUAINTED WITH YOUR NEW PET

Guinea pigs are a constant source of amusement. Every member of your family will be enchanted at the antics of these perky little pets.

Where Do They Come From?

Guinea Pigs are a constant source of amusement. Every member of your family will be enchanted at the antics of these perky little pets.

Apart from a squeaky voice, guinea pigs and pigs have nothing in common. Guinea pigs used to be classified as rodents because of their large gnawing teeth. Today some scientists suggest that guinea pigs be grouped separately. There is agreement, however, that they originate from Central and South America, where they have lived for 35 to 40 million years. Wild guinea pigs were domesticated between 9000 and 3000 B.C., long before Columbus discovered America. It appears that the animals wandered into human settlements on their own, looking for food scraps. At first they were tolerated, and later propagated. The Incas valued them for their meat, as well as for sacrificial offerings to their sun god.

The ancestor of our modern pet is the Tschudi guinea pig from central Chile. There it lives in mountains as high as 12,600 feet (4,200 m). It forms family groups of five to ten animals that inhabit underground caves. Wild guinea pigs look quite different from our sleek pets, because their nutrition, which consists of cellulose-rich grasses and very little water, leads to a marked difference in body structure. However, their basic food requirements and their reproductive biology have not changed significantly.

The International Cavy

Guinea pigs, also known as cavies, spread around the world when traders began sailing the seven seas. Dutch traders introduced the animals to the Netherlands in 1670 as exotic pets for their children. From there the cavies were exported to England and France. As they spread throughout Europe, their appeal grew. They have remained popular ever since.

Where to Find Guinea Pigs

Many pet stores and some breeders sell guinea pigs. You can usually find a variety of colors and fur types. The same sources can usually supply purebred guinea pigs, and at the same time they will advise you on proper care. Another good source of information is a guinea

Your little friend will need a retreat to call its own.

pig show. The location and dates for such shows can be found through breeders, fanciers, and associations (page 62, addresses).

Male or Female?

Males will grow larger and heavier than females of the same strain and are often more lively. When males reach sexual maturity, they exude a somewhat unpleasant smell, which disappears as soon as the animal is neutered.

Females are smaller, and do not exude the unpleasant smell when they mature sexually. They are said to be more affectionate, but that affection probably depends on the nature of each animal, not its gender. Be careful not to purchase a pregnant female (Sexual maturity, page 39).

Sexing young guinea pigs is not an easy task, best left to the experts. Just for your information: males show a space between the anal and the sexual orifice; while these orifices on the female are set very close, the vaginal opening forming a Y-shaped slit.

Attention, Buyers!

Take your time when you are ready to buy a guinea pig. Pay attention to the following pointers:

1. Select a young animal. It is distinctly smaller than the adults, and preferably should be between five and six weeks old. A female that is older than eight weeks may be pregnant (page 34).

2. Guinea pigs are social animals. Observe the animals from which you are going to choose. How do they relate to their siblings?

Lethargic animals who sit quietly in a corner are probably ill.

3. Check the fur carefully. If there is hair loss or thinning hair in patches or all over the body, the animal is either old or sick.

4. Ask to see the teeth of your chosen animal. If the teeth are not properly aligned you are bound to run into health problems later (page 31).

5. Check the feet and nails carefully (page 30).

Note: When you have chosen your pet, take home a small amount of the bedding material from the cage. It will help the little one adjust to its new cage (page 18/19).

How to Pick the One That's Right for You

Healthy guinea pigs show these features:

✔ An overall round, well-padded body with shiny, dense hair

✔ Bright eyes without any trace of secretions

✔ A dry nose

✔ Clean ears

✔ A clean anal area

✔ Tiny feet, which are neat and hairless on their bottom surface

A strawberry is a feast for this tiny creature.

The guinea pig you choose should be lively, alert, and communicative with its cage mates with a variety of sounds.

Sick guinea pigs appear listless, and have dull-looking hair. Do not buy the animal if, in addition, it shows these features:

✔ Sunken flank areas
✔ Watery, red, or swollen eyes, or nasal discharge
✔ Dark, caked deposits on the ears
✔ An anal area soiled with fecal matter

Crisp fresh greens are the undisputed favorite on a guinea pig's menu.

✔ Sore feet, with nails that grow in various directions
Note: In case of evidence of diarrhea, which you can easily recognize by a soiled anal area, do not buy any of the animals from that cage. Diarrhea could be a sign of an infectious disease.

═══ T I P ═══

Legal Issues for Guinea Pig Owners

Leases: If a rental lease does not include any fees or restrictions pertaining to pet ownership, you may assume that the usual house pets are acceptable. This would be particularly true for guinea pigs, since they are not likely to cause damage or to disturb the peace of neighbors. If, however, you intend to keep a large number of guinea pigs, you should check local regulations and ordinances.

Condominium Housing: In most cases guinea pigs are accepted in condo properties, unless the condo association votes for a specific restriction.

Ownership Liability: The owner of a guinea pig is generally liable for any damage his animal may cause to persons or property. If, for example, the guinea pig bites a child, the owner is liable.

Guinea Pig Agreement: A written or verbal purchase agreement is valid. If the guinea pig is sick, the purchaser may return the animal. It is necessary to prove that the guinea pig was sick at the time of the sale. This is not always easy to prove in cases of disease.

Profiles of Guinea Pig Breeds

Currently recognized guinea pig breeds in the United States are Abyssinian, Abyssinian satin, American, American satin, Peruvian, Peruvian satin, silkie, silkie satin, Teddy, Teddy satin, and white crested. The texel and other breeds are gaining increasing popularity, although many are not yet recognized by the American Cavy Breeders Association (see page 62).

Guinea pigs are classified by breed and variety. Breeds are defined by hair type, and varieties by color and markings.

Smooth-Haired Guinea Pigs

The hair is short, smooth, and evenly flat against the body. The color must be uniform over the entire body. Recognized colors:

Agouti: This color resembles the wild ancestral guinea pig color. The grizzled color effect results from the alternating bands of light and dark colors on each single hair, the tip of each hair always being the darkest. Agoutis are bred in gold, silver, cinnamon, and chocolate.

Solid-Color Guinea Pigs: These are usually considered sturdy and healthy. They come in black, chocolate, red, red-eyed orange, lilac, beige, gold, and white.

Multi-colored. Several colors are distributed in various patterns across the body. The resulting color markings are known as brindle, Himalayan, Dutch, tortoiseshell, as well as tortoiseshell and white.

English and American Crested

The animals in these breeds are smooth-haired, carrying a single hair whorl, or rosette, on the forehead. The crest hair of the English breeds are the same color as the body hair.

Recognized colors are agouti and all solid colors, including white. The American crested is marked by a white rosette, and only the colors black, red, gold, and buff are recognized.

Abyssinian

Abyssinian guinea pigs are known for their unique pattern of hair whorls, called rosettes, of which eight to ten are distributed over the body. This special hair growth gives the animals a charming roughed-up appearance. Recognized colors are red, black, white, tricolor, brindle, tortoiseshell, and multicolor.

Rex and Texel

Not yet recognized by the American Cavy Breeders Association (ACBA), *Rex guinea pigs* have hair that is short, fine, soft, and wavy or curly. Recognized colors are red-white, and buff.

Also not yet recognized by the American breeders group, *Texels* are the result of a cross between Rex and Peruvian. Their hair is short and frizzy around the head, but it is long and curled in corkscrews all over the body. Recognized colors are red, and red-white.

Satin

These guinea pigs have particularly silky and shiny hair that is very fine and dense. The satin sheen enhances the intensity of their colors, which are red, gold, buff, cream, and white. Originally bred only as smooth-haired, the satin characteristics are now seen in Abyssinian, Peruvian, crested, shelties, as well as coronets, and teddies.

This little house is as good for sleeping as it is for climbing.

Peruvians

The long, dense, shiny hair of Peruvians grows in whorls all over the body. The recognized colors are red, black, white, tricolor, tortoiseshell, red-multi, and red-black.

Peruvian Silky

The hair texture of the Peruvian silky is like that of the Peruvians, but without the rosettes. Recognized colors are black, red, white, tortoiseshell, tricolor, black-multi, and red-multi.

Note: There are other cavy breeds, like the Texel (fine, soft, wavy or curly hair) which may not have gained ACBA approval, but may be available. You would be well advised to contact the ACBA BEFORE you buy a Guinea pig to discover what breeders and breeds may be in your locale.

P O R T R A I T S :
GUINEA PIGS

The main differences among the many strains of guinea pigs are their colors and fur types. However, cavies with the "wrong" color are just as lovable.

Photo right: Peruvian silky, cream-black-white.

Photo below: Peruvian guinea pig, red; also called Angora.

Photo below: Rex, sepia-white. Its fur coat is short, fine, and silky.

Photo above: Abyssinian, lilac-white-red. The whorls are distributed over the entire body.

Photo above left: A "Dutch" in the normal hair pattern, red and white. Cheeks and hindquarters are of the same color.

Photo above right: Texel, red. The hair is long and curly.

Photo above: White Crested: The single rosette on the head is white.

Photo right: American satin, cream (left), and American satin, red (right). The satin sheen of the fur enhances the intensity of the color.

The Right Housing

For food a guinea pig will gladly climb a ladder.

Guinea pigs demand little in the way of housing except ample space. A large selection of models is available in pet stores.

A single guinea pig needs a floor surface area of 16 × 32 inches (40 × 80 cm).

The bedding pan should have a depth of 4–6 inches (10–15 cm) to prevent bedding spillage. Of course, a cage for more than one animal must be proportionally larger.

While a grated top with access doors appears practical, it allows much of the litter to spill when the animal is scratching vigorously. An acrylic shield prevents the litter from flying about, and gives the animal a full view of its environment, but, inside, the cage may become excessively warm.

Note: Cardboard boxes are unsuitable. They quickly would be chewed up and soaked with urine. For the same reasons, wooden crates are not suitable, unless they are lined with plastic or stainless steel pans.

A Little House to Sleep In

A sleepy guinea pig needs a roof over its head to be a happy camper. The best solution is a box that is a little bigger than the animal and which has an access hole cut in one side. You can choose from a variety of models made of plastic, wood, or bark. Bark is preferable because it gives the animal a chance to use its teeth.

Food Hoppers, Hay Feeders

One or more food hoppers must be in every cage. It is best to use separate hoppers for hay, other foods, and greens, in order to prevent greens from falling on the cage floor and being spoiled by stools and urine. The basic food hopper is usually supplied with the cage; buy additional ones in the pet store. Food hoppers with hinged lids are the most practical because they prevent the guinea pigs from climbing inside the food rack, where they could injure themselves or tear the feeder down.

Containers for Food and Water

Food bowls should be made from glazed stoneware or from porcelain. These materials provide sufficient weight and stability in case the cavies place their paws on the edge of the bowls. Don't choose too large a bowl; you will find your pet sitting in it.

A plastic water bottle with a sipper tube is suspended from the side of the cage. The sipper, which should be made from stainless steel, is bent at an angle for easy access. Your pet will quickly learn its water-dispensing mechanism.

Checklist
of Supplies

1 A cage with a floor space of at least 16 × 25 inches (40 cm × 80 cm) with a bedding pan that is 4–6 inches (10–15 cm) deep, and a grated metal or solid plastic top.

2 Sleeping quarters made of wood or fiber.

3 Three hoppers, one for hay, a second for other foods, and the third for greens.

4 Sawdust (No cedar shavings!) or bio-degradable organic bedding. Under this, a layer of cat litter to help control odor. If your cavy starts nibbling on the litter, use organic materials instead.

5 Food bowls made from glazed pottery or porcelain.

6 Water bottle with sipper tube.

7 Straw to nibble on and to hide in.

8 Comb and brush for grooming—especially for longhaired guinea pigs.

9 Cage furnishings should include a rough stone to keep the nails short, small branches to chew on, and a flower pot to hide in or to climb on.

Gaining Trust

✔ Arriving in its new home, your new pet is likely to be somewhat shy. Keep the area around the cage quiet, and allow the cavy a gradual adjustment period.

✔ Feed the cavy with greens only, and offer fresh water.

✔ Don't change anything inside the cage to speed the animal's feeling of being home and safe.

✔ Do not place the sleeping box into the cage until your pet is fully used to being handled; otherwise it may hide and remain shy.

✔ Ask your children to postpone introducing their pet to their friends.

Taming Your Pet

The first step: Speaking in a soothing voice, gently offer a piece of carrot or apple to your little pet, who will at first only sniff tentatively

Place the cages side by side.

from the safety of its hiding place in the straw. After a short while, the little one will overcome its timidity and will no longer resist getting its treat from your hand.

The second step: When you think that the cavy is used to the smell of your hand, start petting the top of its head with one finger. If the cavy remains still, proceed with gentle stroking of the whole body. Once the animal accepts this without any nervous reactions, you will have gained its trust.

The third step: Now you are ready to gently and slowly reach into the cage. Supporting the body of the guinea pig with your hand

Getting Used to Each Other

If you have two animals who are new to each other, let them see and sniff each other from separate cages at first. Acquainting new cage partners is described on page 21.

under the belly, lift it right onto your lap. Accompany all of your actions by speaking in a low calming voice, and always move slowly. Call the animal's name each time to get its attention, and soon it will be listening for your calls. **Note:** Depending on the individual nature of each guinea pig, these three steps may take varying amounts of time and patience. Do not give up. Be sure to explain the process to your children who are waiting impatiently for their playmate. It is safe to say that even the shyest of cavies will end up eating from your hand.

When Guinea Pigs Remain Shy

Once in a great while a guinea pig may not lose its initial shyness. Maybe an

Guinea pigs love eating from your hand.

experience in its early life rendered it mistrustful. There is only one way to approach a shy guinea pig. Gentle persuasion is the method of choice. Guinea pigs are not aggressive, and they would rather play dead than fight when they feel endangered. Here is what to do:

✔ Take the animal from its cage repeatedly and place it on your lap while stroking it and talking quietly and reassuringly.

✔ Offer all greens and treats only from your hand, and be patient.

✔ Do not place a little sleeping house in the cage;

Hold the animal with both hands against your chest.

rather, add some extra straw in one corner. The animal can easily crawl into this layer of straw for privacy, yet it cannot completely separate itself from the environment.

Discovery Phase
Allow the animal to

"discover" the space it is going to inhabit.

✔ Place your new pet right next to its cage.

✔ Place a tray containing litter close by in case it wants to relieve itself.

✔ Watch where the animal makes his little paths, and mark the route with a few treats.

The Right Location for the Cage

✔ The location should be bright, draft-free, not too warm, and close to family interaction.

✔ The cage should stand on an elevated level of a sturdy table, chest, or sideboard. The floor is unsuitable because of drafts.

What to Avoid:

✔ Direct sun or proximity of heaters or air conditioners

✔ Loud noise, loud music, and smoke

✔ Dark and damp basements

Note: If the guinea pig cage has its place in the children's room, remember to remove it to a quiet area when friends are visiting and there is noisy play. The animals could easily become frightened.

Hay should always be available.

The cage must have plenty of room.

Sipper tubes provide self-watering service.

DAILY HANDLING AND MAINTENANCE

Pet cavies are gentle and affectionate. If you are ready to provide the appropriate loving care and good nutrition, your pet has a good chance for a long, contented life.

The New Home

The trip home should be managed as quickly as is safely possible, with the guinea pig secure in a box or basket. This highly stressful time should be as brief as possible.

When you get home, place the box or basket inside the cage, open the box, and allow the animal to come out at its own pace.

The cage should include: A thick layer of straw or hay, drinking water, a small amount of food pellets in the feed bowl, a quarter of an apple, and one lettuce leaf. The animal is free to hide in the straw and to observe its environment from its hidden and safe location. On pages 18-19 you will find detailed instructions on how to turn the newcomer into a trusting pet.

Getting to Know Cage Partners

It takes consideration and patience to familiarize a new animal with an already

"And who might you be?" Nose-to-nose contact is the guinea pigs' way to get to know each other by scent.

resident older guinea pig. It is strongly recommended that you keep the newcomer in a separate cage for about three weeks, because there is a possibility that disease could be introduced by the new animal.

✔ In the beginning, place the cages next to each other so the animals can get to know each other's scent (see page 18). Later, open the cage doors to allow the animals to visit each other, yet retain their own space.

✔ Take both guinea pigs on your lap at the same time, stroke them gently, and let them discover each other's scent.

✔ Once the animals seem to be adjusted to each other, place them in the same cage. You may want to pet both animals with your hands lightly perfumed. This method removes the dominance of one scent over the other.

Note: Females usually get along very well, although they may fight initially to establish ranking order. This lasts for only a short time. They will soon get used to each other. Once in a while there will be a struggle about who gets to go into the house, but if you offer two sleeping quarters, this problem can be solved. In any case, it is critical that the cage be large enough for two cavy personalities.

Cavies and Children

Guinea pigs are the ideal pets for children. These animals love companionship and want to be cuddled. They become increasingly active as they are stimulated with your attention. However, remember that it takes a little time to develop the necessary trust between the animal and the child. Explain how many things the guinea pig has to get to know, and assure the child that Squeaky will soon wait for cuddles and kisses.

From the start, involve your child in the feeding and cleaning chores. That does not mean that you give up your own overall responsibility for the care and maintenance of the animal. Rather, periodically check that the cavy is happily squeaking, is petted abundantly, and gets the right nutritional foods. Children are often not astute enough to observe behavioral changes that could warn of health problems.

Note: More than a few guinea pigs have been suffocated by children's loving cuddles. These animals sometimes do not fight, bite back, or vocalize their complaint, and they are not agile enough to jump to freedom as a cat would. Your child needs to learn to cuddle the animal tenderly and avoid the potential for injury or death to your pet.

Other Pets

Their natural response to danger is to flee, so guinea pigs are defenseless in captivity. Therefore, you cannot house your new pet with another pet that might consider the cavy an object of prey. Use a commonsense approach to monitoring the company your cavy keeps.

Dwarf rabbits are good companions for cavies. In most cases, the bunny will try to protect the guinea pig, cuddling close to it and licking it. The best combination is a cavy with a bunny that was neutered at an early age. Female rabbits may be tempted to take "ownership" of the cavy, thereby limiting its freedom to venture where it pleases.
Warning: Guinea pigs are extremely sensitive to various antibiotics, which are added to some pet foods, including rabbit pellets. Since healthy animals do not need antibiotic additives in their diets, be sure to read the labels on pet foods carefully, and avoid feeding any of your healthy household animals food that contains antibiotics.

Dogs can usually be trained to accept the company of guinea pigs in the house, especially when they meet as young animals.

Dwarf rabbits and cavies get along, but do not feed your cavy rabbit food, which might contain ingredients harmful to cavies.

If your dog has lived with you for a long time, there must be a gradual adjustment period. Always stay in the same room when introducing cavy to canine. Terriers and other dogs originally bred to kill rats and other varmints are not good choices as guinea pig friends. Some of the easygoing breeds, such as Labrador or Golden Retrievers, might be more amenable to having a guinea pig join the family menagerie.

Cats are likely to look at a guinea pig as prey. Cats can injure or kill a guinea pig if left to their natural instinctive behavior. If you keep guinea pigs on a balcony or in a run in the yard, you need to protect the housing from feline attackers.

A hopper full of fresh hay from a meadow is the "daily bread" of cavies.

Hamsters are best kept alone. In most cases the guinea pigs cannot defend themselves against an aggressive hamster.

Birds often steal the food of their guinea pig companions. Parakeets tend to nibble on a cavy's ears, while parrots and other birds get jealous and attack the gentle cavies.

Guinea Pigs are susceptible to bordetella, so be sure to house them well away from animals that may harbor the organism. Dogs, cats, rabbits, and other pets that have not been inoculated against bordetella should be kept away from your cavies.

The 10 Golden Rules
of Cavy Care

1 Keep your guinea pig with a companion animal from the start.

2 Always speak in a quiet, calming voice, and get the animal used to your hands by offering small treats.

3 To lift your cavy correctly, place one hand under its chest and support the hindquarters with your other hand.

4 Children should hold the animal with both hands against the chest.

5 Never grab the animal suddenly, taking it by surprise. It will develop anxious behavior.

6 Allow your guinea pigs ample free roaming time. They need to satisfy their curiosity and they need physical activity.

7 Be tolerant if your animals do not become fully litter trained. Prepare for their needs by anticipating where they will move, and prepare the quickest cleanup methods.

8 With imaginative cage furnishings you can give your cavies plenty of exercise right in their home.

9 Most important are regular, varied, and high-quality foods. Your little pets should not eat because they are bored; rather, their food should satisfy their physical needs.

10 Keep the cage and all accessories meticulously clean. Dirt encourages the growth of disease-causing bacteria.

The Run of the House

Guinea pigs are lively and quick on their feet despite their roly-poly appearance. They chase each other in wild excitement and jump light-footed over obstacles and hurdles. You need to provide the opportunity for them to run free.

✔ A room with valuable carpets and furniture is not the right place for these exercises, because guinea pigs are likely to nibble on everything, and things may get soiled.

✔ Electrical cords must be out of reach. Cavies could chew on them and the result would be fatal. Telephone cords are also at risk.

✔ Place a flat pan with straw in the same room to serve as a litter box.

✔ Do not leave books and newspapers unattended in the room. Cavies love to chew and play with paper. Even wallpaper is not entirely safe from these rascals.

✔ It is critical that you create an imaginative playscape with lots of corners, niches, elevated blocks (or flower pots), and a variety of small challenges. (HOW-TO: Games and Exercise, pages 48–49.)

Litter Training

Let's face facts: Not every guinea pig can be litter trained. Some animals learn the desired behavior very quickly, others take a lot of time, and the success rate is higher the younger the student begins learning. Here is what to do:

✔ Beginning with the first free run of the house place a pan with cat litter or other cage bedding in the room, and put some of the stool from the cage into the pan.

✔ Every now and then place the animal in the pan.

✔ As soon as the cavy relieves itself somewhere in the room, pick up the tiny balls of stool and place them and the animal in the litter pan.

Provide your pets with shelter from rain, sun, and wind, as well as protection from their natural enemies.

✔ Do not scream or attempt punishment by giving it even the slightest slap. Doing so would achieve the exact opposite of your goal, because it would frighten the guinea pig.

✔ Observe the animal, and check whether it selects a favorite corner somewhere. Place the litter box there.

✔ Every time it uses the litter pan give the animal a treat.

✔ Little puddles on floors or carpets are easily cleaned with clear vinegar or any of the many deodorizers available in pet supply stores. These products remove the urine and the smell. Stool is best removed when it is dry.

Note: If you allow the animal free run of the whole apartment you will need to spread newspaper under beds and cupboards. Remember to block holes and passages to the outside.

Resort Living on the Balcony

If you have a balcony, it is a good idea to create outdoor housing that can be inhabited from spring through fall. Here are some suggestions:

Security: If there is no wall or grate around the balcony, install wire mesh or window screening up to about 30 inches (75 cm) high.

Plywood or other solid materials would provide, in addition to security, protection from drafts.

Protection: Protection must be provided from wind, rain, and direct sun exposure. Insulate the floor with carpet remnants or with natural fiber area rugs.

Cats: Stray cats may be able to reach the enclosure. Secure the top with fine wire mesh or screen in the entire housing. Remember to check whether this is permitted by the condominium or apartment association.

Temperature Fluctuations: If the animal is not kept outdoors year-round you need gradually to condition the cavy to temperature change when you move the animal either indoors or outdoors. In spring, move the animal outdoors at first only during the warm noon hours; otherwise it will catch a cold. Bring your cavy back inside for the night. In the fall do not take it abruptly from the outside into a heated room. Insulate the outdoor housing with Styrofoam and thick layers of straw.

Feeding: As always, feed twice daily with fresh greens and water (page 32–33)
Note: The animal needs sleeping quarters when it stays outside overnight and a litter pan for cleanliness.

Outdoor Housing

If you own a yard or garden you can create part-time or full-time outdoor housing for your beloved cavies. This solution is especially advantageous for cavy groups. The price you pay is some loss of animal–human bonding. You can buy ready-made solid outdoor habitats. The construction has to prevent guinea pigs from getting out and vermin, like rats, from getting in. From above it has to be protected from raptor birds, cats, and badgers. The cavies also need covered shelters from rain, wind, and sun, and solid flooring with water drainage. The roof should be hinged for access so that the straw can be changed easily. Don't forget the drinking devices, and hoppers for food and hay.

This kind of ladder motivates cavies to be active.

Protect Your Pets from Danger

Danger	Source of Danger	How to Avoid Danger
Falling	Balcony Table	Supervise your animals when they run free; secure the area with wire or boards.
Getting crushed or stuck	Doors	Watch carefully when opening or closing doors.
Heat stroke	Sun, heaters	Never place a cage in the sun or next to a heating unit.
Cats Dogs Badgers Raptors	Balcony, outdoor housing	Screen the cavies' housing roof to protect them from their natural enemies.
Electrical shock	Electrical cords, outlets	Unplug nearby cords during free run; cover electrical lines with metal or plaster.
Burn	Any hot objects	Do not allow free run close to stove, toaster, ashtrays, and the like.
Poisoning	Poisonous houseplants, treated or varnished woods	Eliminate poisonous houseplants from all areas where the guinea pig will move about. Use only nonpoisonous paint for housing and furnishings.
Injuries	Human footsteps	Watch your step when the animals run free.
Toxicity from Food Additives	Antibiotics	Read labels carefully. Do not allow cavies access to rabbit food or other pet food that contains antibiotics.

TIP

Problems with Longhaired Breeds

Sawdust is a poor choice for bedding because it sticks to the cavy's long hair. It may be used as a bottom layer for the floor pan, with a second thick layer of straw or hay. Matted hair should be gently parted with your fingers, then disentangled with a broad comb. If the tangles do not yield, cut them off with scissors. Be careful not to touch the skin of the animal. It is a good idea to diminish the incidence of tangles by keeping the hair at floor length. If you want to have the hair at maximum length you may need to keep it on paper rollers.

Note: Guinea pigs can live outdoors year-round, but you must accustom them gradually to temperature changes. Do not move them outside abruptly. Insulate their housing against drafts with Styrofoam sandwiches between plywood, and buffer their housing with thick layers of straw.

Cavy Quirks

Chewing on carpets and on wallpaper: Chewing is part of guinea pig life. This

natural behavior is essential for dental health (page 31). You should compensate for this healthful natural activity by wise design of the cavy's environment. Place valuable papers and books out of reach, block access to forbidden areas, and discourage unwanted activities by clapping your hands. When you catch the animal in the act, grab it and put it back into the cage. Maybe it will remember the connection after a while. Offer ample chewing material: hard bread, twigs, and chewing blocks.

Chewing the cage: Guinea pigs sometimes chew on their cages despite sufficient chewable materials. Maybe the animal is bored and wants to get out. Perhaps the behavior is caused by the presence of another guinea pig. A male could be catching the scent of a female. There could also be two males in separate cages, each getting ready to challenge the other by sharpening his teeth for the showdown. It could just as well be a sign of a little hungry stomach that wants to be fed. Try to get rid of the behavior either by rubbing the cage grate with vinegar or by replacing the framework with a hard fiber material (page 16).

If you seed your own pots, you will always have fresh greens.

Chewing on the sipper tube: Some cavies bring this behavior with them. If you have one of these fellows, remove the sipper tube and replace it with a daily fresh bowl of water.

Fur chewing: When one animal nibbles on the fur of another, it is either bored or it misses rodent "chewables." This is rarely an inherited behavior. Try to change the behavior by offering a variety of chew toys. If all else fails you need to house this cavy with a shorthaired mate, where a little nibble can't do much damage to the "hairdo."

Excessive drinking: When cavies drink too much, they could either have a fever or lack sufficient greens. In the latter case increase the amount of herbs and lettuce leaves (page 33).

A rough stone serves to keep the nails short in the most natural way.

If the little rascal drinks because it is bored, remove the bottle and place it in the cage at specific times for drinking only. Provide adequate play and exercise opportunities.

Loner Behavior: Every now and then, one guinea pig will segregate itself from the others. Usually, this is an animal that has been taken away from its mother early and raised alone. Try introducing this shy cavy to a dwarf rabbit friend, or just allow it to stay in a cage by itself.

Grooming Utensils
✔ Steel comb
✔ Brush with plastic-tipped wire bristles
✔ Soft-bristle brush
✔ Haircutting tool for matted hair

Cavies love the attention of being brushed and groomed. Regular grooming keeps the animal clean, encourages the circulation of blood throughout the skin under the fur, and gives you an opportunity to recognize signs of skin problems or parasites.

Caring for Short and Smooth Fur

Guinea pigs with normal short fur and rosettes need to be groomed twice weekly only during their spring and fall shedding seasons.

Caring for Long Furs

These animals need to be brushed daily. Get your animal used to the procedure at the earliest age. Hold the little cavy on a cloth on your lap and begin by untangling the strands of long hair. Spray some mink oil on the fur before you start, to reduce the painful tug on tangles. Then brush with a soft brush until the hair is shiny. Cut away any matted hair,

Long-haired guinea pigs need to be groomed daily.

especially in the anal area. You can also use untangling shampoo sold for cats, available in pet stores. Dry the hair thoroughly.
Note: Bathe your cavy only when it is absolutely necessary. Use tepid water and a mild baby shampoo. Dry the animal thoroughly and keep it away from drafts because it can easily catch cold.

Clipping Nails

The nails of caged animals grow faster than they can be worn down. Clip them whenever it is necessary. A veterinarian or an experienced pet groomer can show you how to do it right.

Match the cutting profile to the shape of the nail.

✔ Get a proper nail clipper from the pet store so that you avoid splintering the nail.
✔ Inside the nails are blood vessels and nerve endings, which you must not injure. Cut to the point outward from the vessel, and use a slanted cut to match the profile of the nail.

Watch out for the blood vessels.

✔ Be on the safe side; don't cut them too short.

Dental Checkup

Cavy teeth grow constantly and, therefore, require hard foods to chew on to prevent them from overgrowing. Suitable chewables are hard bread, twigs, and chew toys from the pet supply store.

Inherited malocclusion: Unfortunately this condition occurs quite frequently. The poorly aligned front teeth fail to wear adequately and continue to grow. Overgrown teeth must be clipped by a veterinarian every two to three months.

The teeth must be in opposing position for adequate abrasion.

It is all right if the nails are different lengths. If by chance the nail bleeds, press a cotton ball on the nail until bleeding stops.
✔ Inside dark nails it is hard to see where the blood vessel ends. Have someone help you. One person holds the guinea pig and spreads its toes; the other person shines a light from below through the nail and cuts the nail.

Gently wipe the inside of the ear with a tissue.

A Clean Cage

Daily: Clean food bowls with hot water, without detergents.

Twice weekly: Scrub water bottles and sipper tubes with brushes.

Weekly: Clean the cage. Recycle bedding as compost. Kitty litter goes in the trash. Scrub the pan with an ecologically safe cleaner such as vinegar and lemon-based agents. Chemical agents can cause skin irritations. Use brushes and scrapers. Rinse thoroughly with clear water.

Monthly (or more often if necessary): Wash the cage top with hot water.

Cleaning the Ears

Ears must be checked regularly. Remove dust and debris from the ear by gently wiping it with a tissue. Under no circumstances use a cotton swab. If the ears show brown, smelly deposits, ear mites are probably present. The cavy might already show the typical symptom of carrying its head in a tilted position. Consult your veterinarian immediately.

Cleaning the Eyes

Minor secretions in the corners of the eyes can be wiped away with a moistened tissue. Always wipe from the inside toward the outside. If you notice a sudden increase of tearing, there is probably an inflammation or injury, and a veterinarian needs to examine and treat the animal.

HOLIDAY CARE

In-house care: *Cavies are safely left unattended for one or two days if you leave enough food pellets and hay. During a longer absence someone reliable must attend to the animals. Leave detailed feeding and care instructions and the veterinarian's phone number and address.*

Taking them along: *For short trips you can place the animals in a sturdy cardboard box lined with layers of paper and bedding to absorb urine. For extended trips a proper airline-type carrier, available in pet stores, is better. During the trip, the animals must be protected from sun and drafts. Check ahead to see if hotels and motels allow animals. If you travel abroad, make sure to get all necessary border-crossing certificates.*

Note: *Cavies are relatively sensitive to climate changes. Consider carefully whether you want to expose your pet to the stress of traveling.*

Pet boarding: *Friends, responsible family members, and neighbors might help out. Pet stores, and pet boarding facilities, and veterinarians who may board pets are usually not far away.*

Healthful Nutrition

Guinea pigs are not fussy eaters. Early cavy authorities realized that guinea pigs eat a variety of plants, and that they eat everything from the root to the leaves and seeds. It is, therefore, not difficult to feed your cavy. However, these animals do have basic nutritional requirements of proteins and carbohydrates, fats, minerals, and vitamins. Variety is essential. In addition to good nutrition, the animals need exercise. Caged animals will eat more than is good for them if they are bored. If you create healthy exercise options, they will eat only what their bodies need.

Basic Food: Hay

Hay is a cavy's "daily bread." Hay and water can sustain the animal through the winter, if greens become hard to find. Pet stores sell prepackaged hay year-round.

What to watch for:

✔ High quality hay is made from the first cut. It contains clover and young grasses, and its color is pale green. It should have retained an aromatic scent.

✔ Poor quality hay is either old or it lacks nutritious herbs. It is dusty and causes the animals to sneeze. Yellowish, dark-colored, and moldy hay causes disease.

Note: Cavies love hay made from meadow grasses as much as they love clover and alfalfa. Timothy hay is the best, but legume hay is acceptable. Above all, they love hay from weeds and nettles. Legume hay is particularly nutritious, and gives cavies beautiful shiny fur.

Greens, Fruit, Vegetables

Fresh greens, vegetables, and fruit are rich in proteins, calcium, and vitamin C, which are essential for the health of guinea pigs.

Kitchen and garden offer a wide variety of choices: Apples, strawberries, bananas, kiwis, melons, citrus fruit, grapes, green leaf and romaine lettuce, carrots, carrot greens, sweet red peppers, and parsley are nutritious foods. Do not feed any iceberg lettuce or cabbage, and stay away from pears (which cause bloating).

Poisonous are rhubarb, germinating potatoes, and uncooked beans. Also avoid long stalks of celery, which are impossible to digest, and shelled nuts or seeds, which can cause choking. Dairy products cause severe problems, because cavies are lactose-intolerant. Acidophilus powders or liquids are nondairy, and therefore tolerated.
Note: Do not pick wild herbs and grasses where there is much automobile traffic, where chemical sprays may have been used, or where dogs are regularly walked along the side of the road.

Guinea Pig Pellets

Guinea pig pellets are available in pet supply stores. They contain mainly pressed hay and grains, including oats and corn. Stay away from any "guinea pig mixes" if there is any chance that they contain peanuts, sunflower seeds, or other seeds or nuts in their shells. Too many cavies die tragically from choking on shelled seeds and nuts. The high fat content of seeds and nuts is another problem. Pellets may be used as the sole food if you are absent for one or two days. One to two ounces or one to two tablespoons of pellets per day per adult guinea pig contain the right nutritional balance. Feed less if the animal eats a fair amount of fresh greens.

Chewables

Guinea pigs need to chew on hard objects to keep their teeth short (page 31). A variety of chew sticks and similar items are available in pet stores. Hard bread is very suitable. It must be free of chemicals and molds. Twigs, especially from birch, willow, or fruit trees are excellent for this purpose.
Note: Do not use twigs from chemically treated trees. Chew treats that consist of seeds and honey present a choking danger and should be avoided.

Drinking Water

Some people wrongly think that cavies do not need drinking water because they do not see them drink much. Your cavy needs fresh water at all times. The animal chooses when and how much it wants to drink. Chlorinated water should be boiled; bottled water is a better option. Light chamomile tea is also suitable.
Note: Milk, diluted or not, causes diarrhea and must not be fed.

Wash and dry lettuce leaves thoroughly before you give them to your cavies.

Fruit is an essential part of your guinea pig's daily meal.

Vitamins and Minerals

A salt lick stone contains all the necessary salts in the right concentration for your guinea pig. Not all animals will lick it, but you should place one in the cage. Fasten the salt lick to the cage side, off the floor, to safeguard it from urine.

Vitamin supplements are available in pet stores. Only if you are sure that you are consistently feeding a varied, fully nutritious diet may you omit vitamins. During the winter months some of the fruit and vegetables may not be as rich in vitamins as in summer, and you should supplement the regular food. Consult your veterinarian or other cavy expert regarding supplementation.

Cavies and Their Young

Cavies readily present their owners with a new cavy generation. Sows are often pregnant when you buy them, and you have no idea until one day you find four cavies instead of one in the cage. If your children and their friends have guinea pigs, and visit each other with their pets, a new litter may not be far off. Have a plan for what to do with the young before they arrive, or keep only neutered animals.

Breeding Purebred Guinea Pigs

If you want to breed cavies, learn the basic guidelines. The goal is to breed healthy and beautiful animals that fulfill the requirements of the breed standard. A breeder must show the animals in order to get high ratings. Breeding records are essential, and it is best to specialize in specific coat and color lines. For further reading references see page 62.

The parent animals must be healthy, strong, and of the right age. Sows must be at least four to six weeks old. On the other hand, they should not be older than one year. Boars can be bred beginning at six to eight months.

For inbreeding purposes, one pairs the mother with the best male offspring, and the father with the most ideal daughter in the litter. This method usually reproduces the best characteristics in the family. It can, however, also propagate flaws and serious defects.

The basic rules:

✔ Do not breed brothers and sisters.
✔ Half-siblings may be bred provided the parents have no signs of genetic faults. It is important to know the breed stock well.
✔ Inbreeding should be continued only for two generations, because extended inbreeding would enhance negative genetic characteristics.
✔ A new animal should be crossed into the line from time to time.

The Life of Cavy Pairs

The day arrives when you want to pair your little cavy sow with a suitable cavy boar. You anticipate the joy of experiencing their behaviors and watching their offspring develop.

Adjustment period: Do not attempt to place an unfamiliar male with a single female. This could have tragic consequences. If you have a very large cage you can divide it in half with a partition. Otherwise leave them each in their

Checklist
Nutrition

1 Feed the animals at a regular time. They get used to a schedule.

2 Don't offer too much food at once. Except for hay, remove any unfinished foods.

3 Greens, vegetables, and fruit must be fresh.

4 Always place hay and greens in an elevated feeder.

5 Thoroughly wash cucumbers, tomatoes, and fruit, but do not peel them. Bell peppers must be peeled, because the skin is tough. Allow all washed fruit to drip-dry before handing it to the animals.

6 Lettuce must be thoroughly washed and dried to get rid of pesticides.

7 Wash and refill the drinking bottles at least twice weekly.

8 From time to time replace chewable items in the cage.

9 Hand-feed your pets, and let them run free as frequently as possible.

separate cages and place the cages close to each other. Allow the male and female to see and sniff each other. After a few days place them together while you supervise the interaction. Most likely they will begin by trying to impress each other by swatting each other. This is part of their ritual. If they try to bite each other you must separate them for additional adjustment time. If a second attempt to pair them does not succeed, you need to get a different boar.

Note: Before you place the pair together lightly spray your hands with cologne, and pet both animals extensively. This will equalize the scent, and it will distract them from each other's personalities.

Living together: As a rule, pairs live together harmoniously. The boar usually behaves peacefully; if they have a disagreement it is usually the boar who gives in. If he does impose on the sow more than she wants, she gives him a few bumps on the nose, or she might even bite a few hairs from his neck.

The boar tolerates everything patiently, and goes so far as leaving his beloved treats, over which two females or two males would certainly have a fight.

Courting and Mating

Guinea pigs are in heat all year, and mating requires no more than persistent courting by the boar. Males are prepared for this, and circle their intended love with deliberate waddles, seductively swaying rumps, and endless chatter. The sow objects vehemently as soon as he tries to align himself along her flank. She sits on her hindquarters, pushes her front legs straight up, and opens her little mouth wide, showing her wildly threatening little teeth. If this does not impress him sufficiently, she will swipe her teeth across his nose. The boar reacts with a

The little ones wait patiently for their turn at the lunch counter.

squeaking retreat. His courting is not accepted until the little sow is ready to mate. This occurs about every 14 to 18 days. In this interval the ova develop for fertilization. For mating, the female stretches out on her belly, while lifting her little rump in the air. Mating lasts only a few seconds. Right after mating has occurred, both animals begin a thorough grooming session, particularly of the genital areas.

Pregnancy

Gestation takes an average of 68 days until the pups are delivered. At first you will hardly notice the difference in a pregnant female. The

male is especially courteous, always allowing his beloved the best place at the food hopper.

Beginning in the fourth week mom is getting positively plump. No wonder, since the young make up about one half of her body weight now. You can now observe and feel the movement of the pups inside the mother's belly. Surprisingly, the sow shows no indication of nest building. Overall she does not behave differently from any other time, which is the reason why so many unsuspecting cavy owners discover the female's pregnancy very late.

The Birth

Cavy births are usually trouble-free. They usually occur at night, and the owner finds the surprise of the litter in the morning. There are some clear indications of the impending

Shortly after they are born, cavy pups can eat lettuce and other solid foods.

delivery: The female digs in the bedding, vaginal swelling becomes visible, and abdominal contractions are noticeable.

The delivery: The female is in a sitting position when the first pup emerges. She then bites, tears, and eats the membrane that covered the newborn. This allows the baby cavy to breathe. Now the mother licks her pup's nose, ears, and eyes to clean off all secretions. As soon as she is done with the firstborn, the second pup is ready to appear. In most cases there is little blood, and it flows when the placenta is expelled. It is eaten by the sow partially or completely.

Newborn and Independent

Guinea pigs are special in that they are born fully developed. Their eyes are wide open, even 14 days before they are born. Their hair is dense and silky as soon as their dam has licked them clean. The newborn are ready to run and eat solid food, because their teeth developed while they were still inside the uterus. By the time they are two hours old, they rustle about actively but stay close to their dam. They will suckle milk from the sow for only two to three weeks. In addition, they feed on hay and other solid foods. If you end up with orphan pups, you should try to find an adoptive mother. If the latter proves unsuccessful, feed the little ones with feline mother replacement milk. Use a disposable plastic syringe, without needle of course, and slowly introduce the milk into the mouth. Administer about 1–1.5 ml every one to two hours for the first two weeks. Increase to 2 ml in the third week. No feeding is necessary at night.

Note: If you have the opportunity, it is useful to place the growing pups together with some adult animals. It will teach them what to eat. Watch out, though, that an older animal does not try to boss the little one around.

Growth and Development of the Young

Weight: At birth the pups weigh 1.5–3 ounces (40–100g). Beginning after only a few days they will gain one tenth of their weight (4–5g) every day until the fifth or sixth week. Weigh them from time to time. Weight loss is a sign of impending disease, just as in adult animals. If pups lose weight, consult your veterinarian.

Behavior: Baby cavies are truly adorable to watch. A few hours after birth they already groom themselves perfectly. Their dam rarely needs to lick them. Their urge to move around appears to be unbounded. Without a moment's notice they jump straight up in the air, kicking their little feet like acrobats. Then they go on unending chases, speeding in and out of the sleeping box, jumping ecstatically into the air like little goats, and up and over any obstacles as if propelled by springs. This playfulness lasts until they are sexually mature.

Diet: Sows suckle their offspring for about three weeks. Although mom has only two nipples, the pups never fight over their access to the milk fountain, and each waits its turn patiently. In

*Mother and pups eat together,
cuddle up close to each
other, and have lots
to tell each other.*

addition, the young eat hay, lettuce, dandelion, oats, and pellets.

Note: It is essential that the newborn pups eat the cecal stool of their mother. It contains the vitamin B-complex that is essential to their lives, and which cavy pups are not yet able to synthesize on their own. This is nature's practical way of providing for the young!

Family life: Cavy family life is a harmonious affair. The cavies do everything together. They eat together, groom, and cuddle together, and talk endlessly to each other. When they are free to roam, they scurry busily in a long single file, even when they are inside the house. As soon as a little one trails off the track, its long squeaky peep gets mom or dad to come running to get the babe back into line with comforting, reassuring cooing sounds.

Sexual maturity: Females gain sexual maturity at five weeks. If you want to keep them, you need to separate the offspring, by sex, from the parents. Males are sexually mature at seven to eight weeks. Males cannot be kept together in a group because they would start fighting for rank (pages 21, 42).

T I P

Pregnancy Care

A pregnant cavy should not be carried around too much. Teach your children not to cuddle and squeeze their pet; rather have them gently stroke the animal. Mom now needs a diet rich in vitamins—that is, lots of greens. Daily outings are very important because a cavy loves to run no matter how far along in the pregnancy she might be. However, don't chase her at this time. Separate the sow from the boar shortly before the anticipated day of delivery. A female can get pregnant again as early as 12 hours after she has had pups.

BEHAVIOR, FUN, AND EXERCISE

If you provide your little cavy pet with frequent opportunities to run free and a variety of play and exercise options, you will enjoy watching a wide spectrum of behavior.

Survival Instinct

Guinea pigs are defenseless animals, and they must use flight as their sole means of survival. For this, nature has endowed them with speed and agility. Their social behaviors have evolved to be harmonious, and mutually protective.

They develop wide networks of narrow, well-trodden paths, which all pack members know intimately, and which they use for speedy escapes. Cavies move fast even under high grass, and are not easily caught by their predators. Walking in groups they keep close together, one animal behind the other in a long line. The young walk between the adult animals. Cooing sounds accompany the trek, never quite completely stopping. While the clan is grazing, one animal stands guard. At the sight or sound of the slightest change in the environment, the watch animal lets out a squeak, and instantly all the guinea pigs go into hiding.

This guinea pig peers out the door of its house, ever alert to signs of danger. If you don't more gently when you're nearby, your pet will quickly retreat inside its hiding place.

Occasionally an animal might not get into the escape route quickly enough, at which time it will play dead, which often misleads the predator. Last but not least, nature has provided cavies with the most powerful tool of group survival—abundant progeny.

Important Behavior Patterns

The fact that cavies exclusively depend on flight for their survival has equipped them with particular behaviors, which you need to recognize and consider in your interactions.

✔ Like their ancestors, domesticated cavies still display the apprehensive reactions to potential danger.

If you approach the cage suddenly, and, without proper warning, grab into the cage to pick up a cavy, it thinks: "Watch out! Predator!" Since flight is not possible inside a cage, the animal panics. Avoid these experiences by moving slowly and gently when you are near the cage.

✔ Even domesticated cavies are very watchful. The little head jolts forward intently as soon as the slightest unknown movement occurs, and the animal presses itself close to the ground, trying with all its senses, to assess the potential danger.

Life in a Cavy Clan

The social behavior of guinea pigs is very distinct. You will hardly see them jealous or arguing over food. You will notice, however, that there is a strict ranking order within the group. Two males cannot fit into this hierarchical order. The reigning male must prove himself the stronger. In the attempt to gain dominance, the stronger male threatens the weaker one by displaying a wide-open mouth. This is one instance where cavies are tempted to bite. With hackles raised, they begin grinding their teeth noisily, and nasty bites may occur. Once the leader is established, the weaker animal will no longer be tolerated by the clan. He is not allowed at the food hopper, he won't find a place to sleep, and must go elsewhere to make a new life. Females, on the other hand, get along trouble free. However, among themselves females establish a ranking order too, and the lead animals keep order among the young and other adults of the group. In addition, these females take responsibility for the growth and development of the offspring. During the first week of life the young nurse not only from their birth mother but from any other lactating female. If a little one feels lonely, it begins its heartbreaking squeaking, until mom appears to console it. She approaches with a comforting murmured cooing sound, touches the nose of the pup, and leads it back to its family group. Beginning in the second week, the young start to attach themselves more and more to the lead male, whose task it is to wean them from their mothers. They are fully weaned in the third week, at which time there is no more milk available to them.

What to Look For

Caged housing gives guinea pigs no chance to escape in critical situations, which places all responsibility for a smooth cavy group life on your shoulders. Please follow these guidelines:

✔ Young males must be given away by the time they are sexually mature, that is, at around seven to eight weeks. This is necessary not only to avoid fighting but also to prevent uncontrolled breeding.

✔ As soon as you notice that a young male is reduced in the ranking order, you must move that animal to a separate cage. If you don't, the poor animal is left to waste away, since the clan will no longer allow its participation in feeding and group interactions.

✔ If you add a young neutered male animal to a group of females, he may not be able to establish himself as dominant in the beginning. However, as soon as he has gained size and weight equal to that of the females,

Many children's toys provide for play and exercise in the cavy habitat.

his confidence will increase. You can enhance his self-assurance by taking him out of the cage frequently, giving him lavish cuddles, and hand-feeding him.

✔ If one of the animals stays isolated from the group, it might be because it has been kept singly in its earlier life. It may have difficulties in bonding with the others. It may be better for the poor fellow to keep him alone until a suitable companion can be found.

✔ If you must change your cavy group into a new housing complex, no difficulties need be expected. Stress occurs mainly when you add a single animal to an established group, or when a group of cavies must share a space that is too small.

Wood is good for your guinea pigs' teeth. Make sure it is not chemically treated.

Sounds and Their Meanings

If you want to know what your cavy is telling you, keep your ears and eyes wide open. These animals accompany their sound language with specific behavioral patterns.

✔ Insistent squeaking translates unmistakably to begging for food.

✔ Faint or timid peeping and squeaking are the sounds of a fearful and lonely young one. Singly kept cavies use this sound to express their need for human contact.

UNDERSTANDING
GUINEA PIG BODY LANGUAGE

This is "cavy language," which they use among themselves as well as with humans.

 This is the guinea pig behavior.

 What is the animal trying to tell me?

 Now I understand and know what to do!

 Two cavies lying close together.

 The animals need the close physical contact.

 If you keep a single animal, you need to fulfill its need for companionship.

 Two males are fighting.

 The stronger animal is the leader of the clan.

 Place the weaker animal in a separate cage.

 The guinea pigs are touching nose to nose.

 They sniff each other for identification and recognition.

 Allow them ample time to get to know each other.

 The animal is using its nails to remove dust and other particles.

 Healthy guinea pigs groom themselves frequently and thoroughly.

 Brushing twice weekly is necessary only during the shedding season.

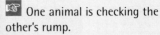 One animal is checking the other's rump.

? If it is a female, he is checking whether she is ready for mating.

! If you do not want offspring, the two should be separated immediately.

The guinea pig extends its head,  anticipating danger.

It is reacting in fear, and ? may panic.

Talk in a calming voice; ! move quietly.

 Your little pet is licking the inside edges of his hands.

? He is washing his little face.

! Make sure the cage is kept meticulously clean.

Reaching for a snack of greens.

? Food stimulates physical activity.

! Keep your pet fit with this kind of exercise.

Mother and pup nose to nose.

? The little one needs close body contact.

! Leave the mother with her young for at least five weeks.

✔ Cooing and gurgling express true contentedness.

✔ Grunting is used for friendly greetings and for nose-to-nose contact.

✔ Growls are voiced by weaker animals towards the stronger ones. The latter may be human. If this fearful growl continues into a chattering teeth behavior you should leave the animal in peace. If you do not respect this warning sound the animal will feel cornered, and might bite in desperation.

✔ Males voice a grunting rattling sound when they are trying to woo a female's attention.

✔ Chirping is rarely heard from domesticated cavies. These are high frequency squeaky sounds that are uttered in pulsating intensity. It is not yet known what elicits these sounds in the wilderness.

Hearing, Vision, Smell, Touch

Hearing is highly developed in guinea pigs. They depend more on their ability to hear than on their vision. They quickly learn to recognize sounds associated with feeding, and they know their human partners from afar just by hearing footsteps. High frequency sounds, which we humans cannot hear, and loud noises are irritating to guinea pigs, and often cause them to panic.

Vision is also very well developed. Their large field of vision enables them to become quickly aware of potential enemy activity in the environment. They are excellent in differentiating colors, particularly yellow, red, blue, and green.

Smell The olfactory sense is most important in initiating sexual contact, differentiation of nonclan members, marking territory, and recognizing familiar humans.

Touch is sensed by the whiskers around the cavies' little mouths. These specialized hairs help the animals to orient themselves in the dark, and to circumnavigate obstacles.

Taste Guinea pigs' sense of taste tells them to stay away from potatoes and onions, two foods they definitely don't like. They love the taste of hay, and seem to like sweet fruit, preferring ripe melon to tart citrus fruit. They will eat just about anything you give them, and will imitate the older guinea pigs. What the grownups like can't be bad.

Guinea pigs are devoted to their grooming habits.

Guinea Pig Language

The Guinea Pig's Behavior	What Does It Mean?
Touching each other's nose	Greeting and acknowledgment
Murmurs, gurgles, grunts	Contentment, comfort, shared feelings
Stretching	Relaxed comfort
Jumping	Happiness, exuberant delight
Squeaking	Pain, fear, loneliness; begging for food (expressed towards humans only); warning
Cooing	Calming sound, reassurance
Sitting or standing up	Begging for food
Standing straight up on all fours	Making an impressive statement of power
Tilting the head up and at an angle	Signaling strength
Lowering the head, growling	Fear; offer of peace
Rattling, hissing, teeth chattering	Aggression, warning the "enemy," trying to impress
Growling, grunting, rattling	Male mating sounds
Mouth wide open, showing teeth	Female rejects male's advances
Stretching the head forward	Watchfulness, alertness
Retracting legs under the body, pressing against a wall	Helplessness, need for protection
Turning rigid	Playing dead to distract the "enemy"

Play Corner

Keep in mind that in their natural habitat cavies develop well-trodden paths under high grasses and branches for their daily livelihood. You can create an extensive playscape consisting of boxes and interconnected toy building blocks. It is important that you rearrange the playscape from time to time and that you add new pieces to stimulate curiosity and exercise. Two animals motivate each other to play, run, and have fun, and a young cavy makes the play more lively.

The Musical Game

Choose an instrument that has a soft sound, such as a recorder or xylophone. Loud instruments will scare your cavies. Play a little tune—the same one each time—when you bring its food. Very soon you will see your clever pet come running to its food bowl as soon as the melody begins.

The next trick to teach your pet is to sit up when you offer a treat, ringing a little bell at the same time. Soon the animal will start squeaking at the sound of the bell and sit up, even without getting a treat.

The Color Game

Get four food bowls, one of each color—red, green, yellow, and blue—and place them about 2 feet (0.6 m) apart. Just before the game begins, put some food in the red bowl. Leave the other bowls empty. One at a time allow a hungry guinea pig to run to the bowls. As soon as the little rascal has discovered the red bowl with the food, pick it up and carry it back to the starting line. After only a few attempts the clever cavy will run straight to the red bowl, no matter where you might have moved it.

Racing

This game is most success-ful if you offer it to several cavies at the same time. Create a web of paths around the room by combining plastic blocks, wood building blocks, cardboard tubes, or

In this playscape guinea pigs can exercise their natural physical and mental abilities.

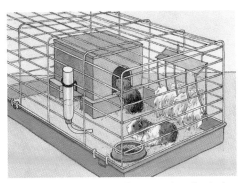

A climb into the sleeping hut provides physical exercise.

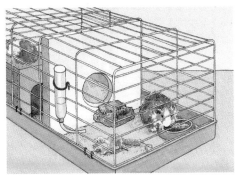

Crawling through a raised hole is required to get to the food.

Activities in the Cage

Many exercises can be performed inside the cage:

✔ Place the sleeping box on a raised platform that can be reached only by climbing a ladder. Or you can place a rough stone in front of the hut so that the animals must climb over it to go to sleep.

✔ Separate the food area from the sleeping quarters by a small board into which you cut a hole at about 3 inches (7.5 cm) from the floor. This provides climbing exercises.

✔ You can create other obstacles by placing twigs or stones in front of the food area. The challenge should be moderate rather than stressful.

✔ Figure out a creative way to suspend the hay hopper, so that the animals must stretch their muscles to reach the food.

✔ Build a structure by combining bricks and a flower pot. While one animal climbs up to hide in the pot, the other enjoys the view from the top.

shoe boxes into a racing course. Now place treats in strategic spots, and let the competitors start their run. Who will reach the lettuce leaf first? The course must be built quite solidly, since the animals will tumble all over the construction to reach the treats. Try to lay out the path so the runners can't see above the obstacles, which forces them to use their noses to follow the scent of the rewards. You will find it amazing how persistent the animals are in their attempts to get to their prized food. Allow your creativity to be limitless!

Note: Remember to change the path of the labyrinth from time to time. Otherwise, your competitors will get bored.

PREVENTIVE HEALTH CARE AND DISEASE TREATMENT

Cavies do not get sick easily. Their natural resistance can be maintained if you feed your pets a healthful diet, give them plenty of exercise, and house them away from animals that might harbor disease organisms to which guinea pigs are susceptible.

An Ounce of Prevention

Healthful nutrition: A good cavy diet is rich in fiber and contains a variety of herbs and vegetables year-round (see page 32).

Cleanliness is important: Soiled cages promote the growth of disease-causing bacteria, which can affect your cavy, other pets, as well as humans. Sanitize the cage and all accessories regularly (page 31), and wash your hands after each of the cleaning chores is done. Teach this to your children from the start.

Health Risks for Humans

Allergies: If you have a tendency to allergies, a guinea pig may activate this condition. If itching or skin irritations occur, consult a dermatologist immediately.

Infectious Diseases Transmissible to Humans (zoonotic diseases): Guinea pigs rarely have diseases that are transmissible to humans, with the exception of skin problems. If you suspect a disease, consult a physician.

Cavies love to stretch to reach their lettuce leaves. This activity exercises their muscles.

Fungal diseases: Humans and animals react with circular itching skin irritations. The animal goes to the veterinarian, and you go to a dermatologist.

Salmonellosis: This is observed not infrequently, and is usually transmitted to children. It requires treatment by a physician.

Lymphocytic choriomeningitis (LCM): Guinea pigs have not been found to transmit this disease.

First Signs of Illness

You are responsible for the early recognition of disorders, and for initiating a course of action (see table, page 55). While a guinea pig cannot tell you how it feels, you can tell by careful observation. If it does not squeak excitedly when you offer fresh greens, if it sits listlessly in a corner, maybe even hunched up, these warning signals should sound an alarm. More serious signs would be a rough coat, hair loss, continued scratching, or labored breathing. These symptoms tell you that your pet is ill.

With minor disorders, determine and discontinue the source of the trouble, and soon your fuzzy pet will be squeaking happily again. Remember though, such a little animal may

need quick and effective help when it is ill. In case of doubt, consult your veterinarian.
Note: Generally guinea pigs do not show signs of illness until late in the course. This is an ancient natural behavior, which prevented them from being cast out from the pack during an early stage of disease. Therefore you need to consider in each case whether you can wait to consult your veterinarian.

What You Can Do Right Away

Minor diarrhea: The overall condition of the animal is still good, but the stool is soft, unformed, and light in color. Remove greens and vegetables and replace them with hay and diluted warm chamomile or fennel tea. Willow branches and grated carrots are also effective. Change the bedding to a thick layer of hay or

Fresh greens are essential to your guinea pig's health.

oat straw. If the stool is not formed after two days of your efforts, you need to get veterinary help.

Straining to defecate: If the anal sacs have accumulated secretions, and the animal is straining, squeeze the area from both sides gently, and use a cotton swab to wipe the contents away. If the stool appears dry and hard, check the water bottle and sipper tube first, in case the animal was unable to drink. Water deprivation is the most frequent cause of constipation. Remove grains from the diet for a few days, and replace them with cucumber and melons. Add to this daily one tablespoon of sauerkraut juice (from a health food store), which you instill with a syringe into the side of the mouth. Gently massage the little belly as frequently as possible. The hay of nettles is also very healing, and so are arugula and dandelion greens. If there is no improvement after 24 hours, you need veterinary help.

Sinus irritation: Remove any potential culprits such as dusty hay or irritating cleaners. If you can't find the cause, consult a veterinarian.

Heat stroke: If you notice that your guinea pig is running nervously to and fro and has rapid or shallow breathing, take it to a shady or cool indoor place without delay and offer tepid drinking water. Make cool compresses and wrap them loosely around the body of the little patient. Then calm the animal with gentle strokes and soothing words.

A Trip to the Veterinarian

Guinea pigs are tolerant little patients who rarely complain about pain. Since the appearance of disease symptoms occurs only in the later stages of disease, it is a good idea not to delay a visit to your veterinarian for too long.

It is best to take your cavy to the clinic in a well-secured cage or carrier (available in pet stores). Do not take the animal out of the carrier in the waiting room. Prepare answers to the following questions to help the veterinarian arrive at a diagnosis:

✔ Where did the animal come from, and how long have you owned it?
✔ How old is the animal?
✔ Which behavioral changes have you noticed, and when?
✔ What does the animal's diet consist of?
✔ Did you change the diet recently?

Checklist
For Good Health

1 Teeth: Hold the animal with one hand under the belly; with the other hand apply just a little pressure to open the little mouth. The upper and lower front teeth should touch, and the molars should form a full bite.

2 Anal area: Clumped and caked fecal matter indicates diarrhea, which may have a variety of causes. The animal must be watched carefully. Clean the area gently with a moist cloth.

3 Skin: Pull the fur apart between two fingers. Inflamed areas and hair loss are indications of parasites. Fungal infection causes circular hairless lesions. Consult a veterinarian immediately.

4 Ears: With a flashlight, check external and internal ears. Increased scratching is a sign of a problem. Ear mites cause brown, crusty, bad-smelling deposits and red inflamed areas inside the ear (otitis).

TIP

Weight-Loss Diet

If your cavy gets a little too fat, put it on a diet. Overweight animals become lethargic and are more susceptible to diseases than are lean animals. Reduce or remove treats and stay consistent no matter how cute your darling's begging. Feed about 1.5–3 ounces (40–60 g) greens per day, and reduce the regular diet to 0.7 ounces (20 g) per week. Instead of bread give small untreated branches to nibble on, and let your roly-poly run free as much as possible. Encourage the animal to exercise by holding the lettuce high to induce reaching or by moving the food higher in the cage to prompt climbing.

Overweight animals are more prone to diseases than their lean cagemates.

✔ Have stool and urine shown any signs of change? Take samples.
✔ Describe the environment of the cage at home.
✔ Did the animal have physical contact with other guinea pigs?

Be meticulous in following veterinary instructions and administer medications correctly and consistently. Do not lose your patience if the recovery is prolonged. Your little patient will reward you generously for your perseverance. Detailed nursing tips are on pages 58-59.

The Guinea Pig Refuses Food

On occasion a sick guinea pig will stop eating altogether. Whether or not its appetite can be restimulated by force-feeding must be determined by a veterinarian. There are a variety of potential causes for this problem.

✔ Problems with the alignment or growth of their teeth cause guinea pigs to be unable to eat (page 31). When the dental alignment is off, the teeth grow unhindered, rendering the animal unable to take in any foods. As soon as you notice a lack of appetite, seek veterinary treatment to prevent the cavy's starvation.

✔ Guinea pigs can suffer severely from the loss of a cage mate, and literally starve themselves to death. Instead of forced feeding a new companion animal would be a better cure.

Euthanasia

If your beloved pet suffers from a painful or incurable disease, it may be merciful to provide a humane death. When considering the options, you may also think of the fact that all animals basically want to survive. In older animals particularly, most health problems arise over time. They may be used to a certain discomfort as long as there is no pain. It is a good idea to get your veterinarian's advice for

Recognizing and Treating Disease

Symptoms	Treat at Home	Consult a Veterinarian
Sits around listlessly, no squeaky greeting	Boredom, lack of companionship, lack of affection, or exercise	Apathy, loss of appetite, diarrhea, weight loss, unthrifty hair coat
Refusal to eat adequately	Inappropriate or spoiled foods, lack of fresh water, soaked bedding, draft, room too cold or too warm	Foul-smelling diarrhea sometimes mixed with blood, hunched-up posture, apathy, dried nasal secretions
Excessive salivation, caked secretion in the lower jaw area	Insufficient use of the teeth, chewing materials needed (page 31)	Skin irritation, hair loss, scabs around the mouth area, food refusal
Diarrhea	Change in diet, food or water too cold, environment too humid or too cold	Food refusal, weakness, sunken eyes, apathy, wasting, emaciation
Unsuccessful attempt to defecate or urinate	Lack of exercise, defective drinking bottle, sudden change from greens to dry foods	Fever, dragging hind limbs, spasms, difficulties breathing
Sneezing, coughing	Draft, irritation from reaction to bedding, reaction to cleaning agents, dusty, or spoiled hay	Apathy, lack of breath, nasal discharge, weight loss
Watery eyes, red or swollen lids	Dust or foreign particles, injury from scratching, irritation from hairs reaching into the eye area.	Sensitivity to light, conjunctivitis with swelling and reddening, bulging eyes
Accelerated breathing	Overheating, fear, stress	Inflating the cheeks, flank breathing, bluish gums
Increased scratching	Lack of sanitation, poor grooming habits (matted hair)	Scabs, ulcerations, cramping, head tilting
Lameness, unwillingness to move	Nails too long, wrong bedding (e.g., use of cat litter)	Dragging hind feet, inability to bear weight on hind legs, balance disorders
Minor bleeding	Superficial skin lesions	Spasms, bite injuries
Areas of hair loss	Lack of vitamins, hair biting due to lack of roughage/fiber in the food	Round hairless spots, bilateral symmetrical hair loss

the decision on when to euthanize. Whatever
the cause of death, the loss of a beloved pet is
sad and heartbreaking. This moment of good-
bye is especially difficult for children, and it is
up to you to take time for explanations and to
help deal with the sorrow.

Note: Many pediatricians are overprotective
about infectious diseases that are transmissible
from pets to humans. Do not put a guinea pig
to sleep based only on a suspicion. It is the
place of a veterinarian to give the determining
information, and, where necessary, to advise
the person's physician.

When a Guinea Pig's Companion Dies

In most of these cases the remaining animal
becomes depressed, sitting around, and refusing
food. Even if the animal continues eating, you
need to understand that it is sadly affected by
the loss. In any case, it is best to get a new
companion soon. A young guinea pig of about
six to ten weeks would be the easiest acceptable
choice. Introduce them gently, and proceed
according to the steps described on page 18.

*A guinea pig that lacks an appetite is
not well.*

Note: Do not try to replace the companion
yourself. In the long run you cannot fulfill the
needs of your pet, and the animal will suffer
the consequences.

*Companionship is an essential ingredient
for the health of your guinea pigs.*

Proper Housing

As a preventive measure, isolate the sick animal in a separate cage. If you suspect an infectious disease, you need to change the bedding frequently and disinfect all utensils and cage parts. Place the cage with the sick animal in a separate room, which should be warm, quiet, and not too bright. Keep frequent affectionate contact with the animal to prevent it from being lonely in addition to being ill.

Guinea pigs do not vocalize to express pain. They depend on your observation to notice changes in their expression and body posture to tell you how they feel. The more attentive your care the better your animal will respond.

Disinfecting the Cage

Most disinfecting chores should be done with an organic disinfectant. Some are made from orange oil or other natural products. If you suspect a serious infection, consult your veterinarian for the most effective agent and methods.

Liquids are administered with a syringe (without needle) or a plastic dropper.

Place the tip of the syringe from the side through the space between the teeth.

Drinking

The sick animal must take in liquids to prevent dehydration. Use a syringe (without needle) to slowly instill water into the side cheek pocket. Administer small amounts drop by drop, seeing to it that the animal has time to swallow the fluids.

Carefully clip away the hair before you dress a wound.

Applying Ointments

In cases of small lesions, snip away the hair around the lesion. Clean the wound carefully with chamomile tea, and follow by applying a

Infrared lighting may be used to aid recovery in some cases. Make sure the light covers only a small area of the cage so that the animal can choose a cooler area if it is too warm. **Hold your hand under the lamp to check how much warmth is radiated.**

The light should affect only a small section of the cage.

thin layer of calendula ointment. Wait for the dressing to dry before you place the animal back in its cage. The animal would instinctively lick the freshly applied ointment off the wound.

Carefully dab the corners of the eyes.

Eye Treatments

If you need to treat swollen or red eyes use chamomile tea to dab the corners of the eyes; better still,

use prescribed eye drops that do not sting. Place the animal in a room with dimmed lights until the inflammation has disappeared.

What to do for Allergies

The cause of the allergy has to be determined by a veterinarian before you can act.

✔ If hay is the problem, put just enough hay in the feeder for one meal.

✔ If the bedding material is the cause, change to an organic hypoallergenic bedding.

✔ If one food, such as salad greens, is the culprit, remove that particular food from

the menu. Remember to remove any potential allergenic offenders from any accessible outdoor area.

Strengthening Weak Animals

If you encounter an otherwise healthy animal that appears weak, increase the quality of greens and add wheat germ, vitamins, herbs, and oats. Allow as much outdoor activity as possible, yet avoid excessive exercise and drafts. Ask a veterinarian for an injection of general strengthening agents. Do not use this animal for breeding.

Presurgical and Postsurgical Care

Healthy animals recover easily from surgeries such as spaying or neutering. Begin daily doses of vitamin C at one week prior to the surgery. Lack of vitamin C is known to prolong postsurgical recovery time. Do not feed the animal for 12 hours before the procedure. After the surgery, keep the animal quiet and warm, and do not feed it until 12 hours have passed. **Do not remove the water either before or after surgery.** Offer the best foods available in order to speed recovery.

A bell pepper should be peeled because its skin is hard to chew.

Helpful Addresses

For information on location of regional clubs, shows, and standards:

American Cavy Breeders Association (ACBA)
Walter Linker, Secretary-Treasurer
3034 Forest Oaks Drive
Orange Park, FL 32073
(904) 278-8150
wlinker@bellsouth.net

American Rabbit Breeders Association (ARBA)
1925 S. Main Street, Box 426
Bloomington, IL 61704

Both clubs offer newsletters and guidebooks with information and references.

Helpful Books

The Proper Care of Guinea Pigs, by Peter Gurney, 1997, TFH.

Raising a Healthy Guinea Pig, by Wanda L. Curran, 1997, Storey Comm. Inc.

The Guinea Pig: An Owner's Guide to a Happy, Healthy Pet, by Audrey Pavia, 1997, Howell.

The books and newsletters of the breeders associations have the best and most current information.

The Internet

The most complete and up-to-date information is found on the 'Net: For details on anything about cavies, surf the 'Net. Conduct a World Wide Web (www) search on your computer for *cavies,* and proceed from there.

The Author
Katrin Behrend, a journalist and an editor of books about animals, lives in Germany and Italy. Guinea pigs are one of her areas of specialization in the field of pet care.

The Artist
György Jankovics studied graphic design in Budapest and Hamburg. He is a renowned illustrator, specializing in animal and plant subjects.

The Photographer
Karin Skogstad has worked as a freelance journalist and photographer since 1979. Animals and plants are her areas of special interest.

Photos
Page 1: Rex (left) and Red and White Alpaca (right). Pages 2 and 3: Shorthair spotted. Pages 4 and 5: Satin, Solid Red (top), American Crested Satin, Solid Cream, (bottom). Pages 6 and 7: Rex, Rosette, Texel, Sheltie (from left). Page 64: Satin, Solid Red (left) and Longhair Lilac (right).

Important Note
This Pet Owner's Manual tells the reader how to buy and care for guinea pigs. The author and the publisher consider it important to point out that the advice given in the book is meant primarily for normally developed guinea pigs from a good breeder; that is, guinea pigs of excellent breeding, temperament, and physical health.

Anyone who adopts a guinea pig from a shelter or an owner who can no longer keep it should be aware that the animal has already formed its basic impressions of human beings. The new owner should watch the animal carefully, including its behavior toward humans and other animals, and, if possible, meet the previous owner. If the guinea pig comes from a shelter, it may be possible to get information on its background there. Before taking it home and introducing it to other household pets, the new owner should take it to a veterinarian for a health check.

Guinea pigs sometimes have diseases that are communicable to humans. If your pet shows any symptoms of a disease, consult your veterinarian immediately. If you have questions about your health, see your doctor without delay.

Questions on guinea pig maintenance can be answered by most pet store personnel. There are also a variety of breeder groups who are usually willing to answer your questions. Last but not least, there are many interested parties on the Internet who are glad to answer questions.

English translation © Copyright 1998 by Barron's Educational Series, Inc.

Original title of the book in German is
Meerschweinchen

Copyright © 1997 by Gräfe und Unzer Verlag GmbH, München
Translation from the German by Helgard Niewisch, DVM

All inquiries should be addressed to:
Barron's Educational Series, Inc.
250 Wireless Boulevard
Hauppauge, New York 11788

http://www.barronseduc.com

Library of Congress Catalog Card No. 98-18038

International Standard Book Number 0-7641-0670-8

Library of Congress Cataloging-in-Publication Data
Behrend, Katrin.
[Meerschweinchen. English]
Guinea pigs : everything about purchase, care, nutrition, grooming, behavior, and training / Katrin Behrend ; photographs by Karin Skogstad ; illustrations by György Jankovics ; [translated by Helgard Niewisch].
p. cm. — (A complete pet owner's manual)
Includes bibliographical references (p.) and index.
ISBN 0-7641-0670-8
1. Guinea pigs as pets. I. Title. II. Series.
SF459.G9B4313 1998
636.935'92—dc21
98-18038
CIP

Printed in Hong Kong
15 14 13 12 11

The experts answer the ten most frequently asked questions on guinea pig care and maintenance:

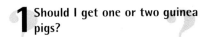

1 Should I get one or two guinea pigs?

2 Do males get along with each other as well as females do?

3 Do I have to get permission from my landlord to keep guinea pigs?

4 Should I get my guinea pig from an animal shelter?

5 Where can I find purebred guinea pigs?

6 Are guinea pigs expensive?

7 What should I watch out for when I am ready to pick my pets?

8 Can I train my guinea pig to use the litter box?

9 Will my guinea pigs bite me?

10 May I feed leftovers from my meals to my guinea pig?

Guinea pigs are highly social animals. They are happier when they are not alone.

Males get along fine, as long as they are neutered before their sexual maturity and as long as they were housed in groups at an early age.

Check your rental contract. In most cases there is no formality necessary if you keep only a few clean, quiet animals.

It depends on how long the animal has been in the shelter. The longer it has been removed from personal attention, the harder it may be to resocialize it. Take it directly to your veterinarian for a health check.

The American Cavy Breeders Association (ACBA) can supply you with the necessary information (page 62).

Prices for guinea pigs vary as much as the variety of strains and vendors. Take time to compare!

The animal should appear healthy and alert, the teeth should be properly aligned, and the nails should not be too long.

This is a question of your patience and of guinea pig character. Not everyone is successful.

When your guinea pig is scared it expresses this by growling and by chattering its teeth. If you do not leave it in peace it might try to nip your finger. It is also not wise to try to use your hand to separate two fighting cavies.

Guinea pigs are herbivores, and as such need fresh greens and food that is rich in cellulose. They enjoy fruit peelings, and leftover vegetables, but will not do well with more than an occasional meal of human salad.

Information and advice to help you take good care of your guinea pig

Guinea pigs make interesting and lovable household pets. Both children and adults will enjoy keeping these animals and observing their activities.

The typical guinea pig: its life cycle, temperament, origins, and more

Expert advice: feeding, health care, breeding, housing, activities

Understanding your guinea pig: how it expresses its needs in vocal and body language

Step-by-step directions cover everyday care of your guinea pig

Informative and attractive charts, tables, and sidebars

Filled with handsome full-color photos

ISBN 0-7641-0670-2

UPC

0 27011 00670 8

BARRON'S